What to do when your mom or dad says . . .
"DO YOUR HOMEWORK!"
(AND SCHOOLWORK)

By

JOY WILT BERRY

Living Skills Press
Fallbrook, California

Distributed by:

Word, Incorporated
4800 W. Waco Drive
Waco, TX 76703

CREDITS

Producer
  Ron Berry

Editor
  Orly Kelly

Weekly Reader Books edition published by
arrangement with Living Skills Press.

Dear Parents,

"DO YOUR HOMEWORK!" — Do you remember how you felt when your parents said this to you? If you are like most people, your remembrance of the occasion is not a positive one. Homework and schoolwork ... both of these are words that evoke a certain kind of negative response from many of us. The question is why? They are only words ... words that are neither good nor bad in and of themselves, words that have no real power or control. Why, then, do many of us cringe at the mere mention of them?

Could it be that homework and schoolwork, originally intended to be educational aids, have become disciplinarian aids used to get students to "shape up" or "toe the line"? The answer to this question may be found in well-worn threats such as: "You'd better be good in school today or I'll give you a lot of homework!" or "No playing until your homework is done!"

The misuse of homework and schoolwork intensifies the problems parents and educators face in educating children, feeding the tension and stress that are counterproductive to the educational process.

Unfortunately, some adults overreact to this situation by "throwing the baby out with the dirty bath water." They do away with homework and schoolwork altogether, hoping to alleviate the problem which in reality may put the educator and student at a disadvantage.

What can be done about this? If homework and schoolwork are to help instead of hurt, several things need to happen. Parents, educators and students must:

1. Redefine the purpose of homework and schoolwork, making sure that they are seen as educational, **not** disciplinarian, aids.

2. Commit themselves to the accurate definition.

3. Develop educational programs in which students are personally involved in using homework and schoolwork to further their own education.

4. Equip the students with practical skills that will enable them to get the most out of homework and schoolwork.

This book can help bring about these four things. If you use it systematically as a part of a continuing program, or as a resource to be used whenever the need for it arises, you and your child will experience some very positive results.

With your help, your child can and will begin to assume responsibility for his or her own education so that one day you will not have to say, "DO YOUR HOMEWORK!" at all.

Sincerely,

Joy Wilt Berry

Has your mother or father ever told you to . . .

When you are told to do your homework, do you wonder ...

If any of this sounds familiar to you, you're going to **love** this book.

Because it will explain the purpose of homework and tell you how to get it done as painlessly as possible.

To understand the purpose of homework and schoolwork, it is important to understand the purpose of schools. The purpose of most elementary schools is to teach children the things they need and want to know in order to survive and grow.

To help children learn the things they need and want to know, schools have them do schoolwork and homework.

If you think carefully about some of the things you have learned, you will find that they fit into two groups.

The first group is *instant knowledge,* and the second is *knowledge through practice.*

Many of the things you know, you have learned immediately after you have experienced them. For example, when you touch a hot stove, you learn right away that the stove is hot and can burn. You don't have to touch the stove over and over again to learn this. This is called instant knowledge.

But think about learning to tie your shoelaces. If you are like most people, someone showed you how to tie your shoelaces; but you had to do it over and over again before you really knew how to do it on your own. This is called knowledge through practice.

Schoolwork (the work you do in school) should help you get both instant knowledge and knowledge through practice.

Schoolwork that encourages children to **explore** often helps them gain immediate insight.

To explore means that you try to find out about something by investigating it. You study it. You examine it carefully.

One way to explore is to observe. When you observe something, you look at it closely. You watch it carefully.

Another way to explore is to experience it. When you experience something, you feel it, listen to it, taste it (if it is something you can eat) and smell it.

Another way to explore is to research. When you research something, you ask questions or read about it.

Another way to explore is to experiment. When you experiment with something, you work with it, trying it out and testing it.

Knowledge through practice is gained by doing something over and over again until you can do it easily, correctly and on your own.

Knowledge through practice is also gained by memorizing, which means thinking the same thought over and over until it becomes an automatic part of your thinking.

To get the most out of school, you need to have a chance to learn both instant knowledge and knowledge through practice. Therefore, it's important that your schoolwork involve:

observation,	experimentation,
experience,	practice, and
research,	memorization.

Think about the things you do at school. Do they include all of these things?

	List the activities that accomplish each thing
OBSERVATION	
FIRST-HAND EXPERIENCE	
RESEARCH	
EXPERIMENTATION	
PRACTICE	
MEMORIZATION	

If any of these things are missing from your schoolwork, you might want to talk to your parents and teacher about it. They might try to see that it will be included in the schoolwork you do.

If you are like most children, you enjoy doing one kind of schoolwork more than others. You may want to do the schoolwork you like all the time and avoid doing what you don't like.

If this is true, you need to know and remember that learning often requires doing some things you do not much enjoy doing.

When you are faced with schoolwork you do not want to do, there are several things you need to avoid.

AVOID PUTTING IT OFF.

If you have schoolwork you don't like, do it as soon as you can.

Get it over with so that you can do the things you want to do.

AVOID FOOLING YOURSELF AND OTHERS.

Do what you say you will do. If you tell yourself or someone else you're going to do some schoolwork, do it!

Losing trust is one of the worst things that can happen to you. It's sad when other people can't trust you, but it's even sadder when you can't trust yourself.

AVOID ESCAPING.

Don't try to get out of doing schoolwork by doing something else. There are many ways you may try to escape schoolwork. Here are a few of them:

DOING THINGS THAT HAVE NOTHING TO DO WITH WORK

DAYDREAMING

GOOFING OFF

There are two things you can do to help yourself do your schoolwork.

One is to **play a game** with yourself. Set yourself a time limit and try to get the job done in that amount of time.

The second thing you can do is to **reward yourself.** Promise yourself that you will do something you really want to do after you've finished.

And make sure you keep the promise you made to yourself.

There are some old sayings that will be helpful for you to know as you do your schoolwork.

1. **HASTE MAKES WASTE.** This means that when you hurry too much, sometimes you end up spending more time on a job. Often when you hurry or rush, you have an accident or make mistakes.

35

2. ANYTHING WORTH DOING IS WORTH DOING RIGHT.

This means if you are going to take the time to do something, you should do it well. Otherwise you should not do it at all. Doing a bad job is a waste of time.

3. ONE STEP AT A TIME.

This means whenever you have a lot of schoolwork to do, you need to do one thing at a time. Nobody can do everything at once.

4. FIRST THINGS FIRST.

This means you need to do the most important thing first, and the rest in the order of their importance. You may want to ask your teacher to help you decide what order to do them in.

41

Sometimes there isn't enough time for you to learn what you need to know while you're at school.

When this happens, you may decide or your teacher may ask you to do some work at home. Work from school that is done at home is called homework.

THE ARGUMENT FOR HOMEWORK

Different people have different opinions about homework. Some people think that homework is absolutely necessary if children are to learn everything that they are expected to learn. People who think this way often feel that the things children learn at school must be practiced at home if they are to be learned well. These people also feel that homework is a good way to get children to discipline themselves and be responsible for doing things on their own. Therefore, these people think that homework is a necessary part of a child's education.

THE ARGUMENT AGAINST HOMEWORK

Other people believe that children who have been in school all day need a break from schoolwork. These people say that most adults are not expected to take their work home, so why should children? These adults also feel that what children do after school, the games they play, the friends they make, are very important and should not be interrupted by homework. They also think that homework can unnecessarily make children and their parents angry at each other.

What does your teacher think about homework? Is he or she for or against it? Why?

What do your parents think about homework? Are they for or against it? Why?

What do you think about homework? Are you for or against it? Why?

If you don't all agree, it's important that you talk the issue over and come up with an agreement that all of you can live with.

If it is decided that you should do homework, it's best if you do it the FIRST THING when you get home from school. This is so that:

1. You won't forget to do it.

2. It won't interfere with your after school activities. You will enjoy doing what you want to do much more if you don't have to think about the homework you should be doing.

3. The homework will be done, and you will be free to do other things as they come up.

Also, when your homework assignment is finished, put it in a place where you will be sure to remember to take it to school with you the next day.

For example:

If you take a lunch box, book bag, or bike pack to school, put your homework in there.

If you wear the same jacket or sweater every day, put your homework with the jacket or sweater.

Put your homework by the door so you will remember it as you leave for school.

THE END of unfinished homework and schoolwork!